THE LAGOM LIFE

THE
LAGOM LIFE
A Swedish Way of Living

balance • harmony • beauty • sufficiency

ELISABETH CARLSSON

CICO BOOKS
LONDON NEW YORK

For my parents, who have inspired me more than they will ever know.

First published in 2017. This edition published in 2023 by CICO Books
An imprint of Ryland Peters & Small Ltd
20–21 Jockey's Fields, London WC1R 4BW
341 E 116th St, New York, NY 10029
www.rylandpeters.com

10 9 8 7 6 5 4 3 2 1

Text © Elisabeth Carlsson 2017, 2023
Additional text and makes © Fiona Bird (pp84–85), Willow Crossley (pp102–103, 116–19, 158–61) and Emma Hardy (pp29–30)
Illustration © Clare Youngs 2016, 2023
Cover illustration © Ivanna Ivashka/Adobe Stock
Design © CICO Books 2017, 2023
For photography credits, see page 175.

A CIP catalog record for this book is available from the Library of Congress and the British Library.

ISBN: 978-1-80065-185-2

Printed in China

Editor: Marion Paull
Recipe copy-editor: Gillian Haslam
Designer: Louise Leffler
Lifestyle photographer: Gavin Kingcome
Stylist: Nel Haynes
Recipe photographer: Stephen Conroy
Recipe stylist: Tonia Shuttleworth
Home economist: Tamara Vos
Illustrator: Clare Youngs

Senior editor: Carmel Edmonds
Art director: Sally Powell
Head of production: Patricia Harrington
Publishing manager: Penny Craig
Publisher: Cindy Richards

contents

introduction

While I was growing up in Sweden, I didn't really question lagom, the idea of living with consideration for others, and doing things simply and practically. The word was part of everyday life. Essentially, it's about balance. Lagom was how my mother served dinner, and how she explained the temperature of the lake — lagom warm (mostly too cold in my view, back then). Lagom also meant staying within social norms, which, of course, as a teenager felt restrictive. Now I realize my relationship with lagom was complicated, and I guess that's true for most Swedes, probably more so than we care to admit.

Age 19, I rebelled against being "just lagom" and moved to Madrid, where life was completely different — it was loud, people were open and opinionated, and they didn't try to hide their emotions. I loved the culture shock. But in Spain and elsewhere, I carried lagom with me. A quiet affinity existed between us ex-pat Swedes about how to do things the lagom way. We had probably all moved abroad to get away from it, but with distance, lagom had become something we were comfortable with and recognized. We wanted to have lagom but our version of it — not showing off or grabbing too much of the spotlight but still celebrating when things went well, being happy for each other and ourselves, and knowing it's okay to be different, because actually we are all part of an interconnected whole.

With age, I understand that lagom is a key part of having a healthy and balanced journey in life. So much of who I am, my views, my beliefs, my

decisions, are guided by this sentiment, and it explains a lot about why I reacted as I did, both at home, pushing against it, and abroad, being guided by it. Perhaps the lagom of my childhood didn't suit me. As an adult, having found my own equilibrium, I have developed my own sense of lagom, which I can appreciate and apply to my own life. Living the lagom way doesn't mean a safe life. You can still take risks, just lagom risks!

The lagom I live by today comes with acceptance, inclusion, laughter, love. It recognizes difference, sees possibilities, yet seeks to include, to encourage, and it can be applied to every aspect of life.

chapter 1

lagom—
what does it mean?

It evokes contentedness, having enough
and not feeling deprived.

way of life

Lagom is a quintessentially Scandinavian concept that is now becoming a trend outside Sweden, to the surprise of us Swedes. As far as the rest of the world is concerned, it means "not too much, not too little, but just about right." It doesn't mean "not enough," or imply frugality. If you have any interest in learning the Swedish language or understanding Swedish culture, you could do worse than learn about lagom.

First, let's start with how it's pronounced — and let's try to leave the Muppets' Swedish chef out of it please! Try "law-ghum" or "lah-gum" and Swedes will get the idea. The word itself dates back to between the 8th and 11th centuries when we all wore funny hard hats with cow-horns attached and called ourselves Vikings. The story goes that a communal horn filled with *mjöd* (a fermented honey wine) was passed *laget om* (around the group) and each person took just a small sip so there was enough for everyone — and so the word lagom was born. Others say it derives from the Swedish word *lag*, meaning "according to the law," but I prefer the Viking story myself.

only a useful word or something else?

Lagom is not only a useful word in Swedish, but could also explain a lot about how Swedes behave. Lagom can be applied to many things — how much ice cream you want, the size of your house, the spiciness of a salsa, how drunk you got last Friday (yes, really!) — but lagom signifies value as well as quantity. The philosophy of "just right" translates into moderation, a sense of balance and togetherness.

Ben, an Englishman living in Sweden, tells me he "never really understood the fuss [about lagom]. It doesn't exist . . . in English but I don't see it as a concept or as something Swedish, but rather as a good word. It means just about right, an unspecified but appropriate amount. How much sauce do you want? *Mehhh, lagom tack.* Then you get served a normal amount."

still good value?

From searching for "lagom" on various Facebook "Swedes abroad" forums, it's clear that, even though we may not live in Sweden or speak the language on a daily basis, we ex-pats use the word a lot. However, can we still assume that everyone knows what we mean when we use it as a value statement?

That might be a generational thing. If you were born after Sweden gave the world the band Ace of Base in 1992, your idea of lagom might be very different from how those of us who preceded that time interpret it. The detractors of lagom often mention how it can be very "middle of the road" and stifling if you fall on either side of that road. A parallel can be drawn with Sweden's popular 1.5 percent milk, *Mellanmjölk*, which has been sold in the same green cartons since the 1980s — just creamy enough, not too light or too fatty. *Mellanmjölk* was the name of stand-up comedian Jonas Gardell's tour when he burst onto the scene in the 1990s. His colorful personality was not to everyone's taste and he was definitely not lagom by Swedish standards. However, the enormous success of his tour bears testament to how many people did identify with the feeling of being a square peg in a round hole, and having the conformity of lagom bearing down on them in every aspect of life. So, does lagom fit in another era when Sweden was more homogenous and insular? With globalization, social behavior is changing and perhaps the old ideas no longer suit our culture, in which case they will have to evolve along with the rest of society.

a new kind of lagom

It seems to me that lagom is reinventing itself. In a world that, according to the news anyway, seemingly teeters on the brink of catastrophe every day, and in which the divisions of wealth are getting bigger across the globe, the concept of balance, collectiveness, and frugality over instability, individualism, and greed is quite an attractive proposal. Just being lagom might not solve global warming and world hunger but isn't it important for each of us to do what we can to contribute to the world we live in?

Lagom is a philosophy that we can all learn to live with for the sake of our own wellbeing and that of the planet. Think about consciously reducing your impact on the world, whether that's by recycling or reducing your energy bill. Don't take out more than you need. Lagom might be a passing trend but the ethos that supports it can serve as a guiding principle for all of us and for future generations.

Swedes know happiness, and much of it is down to lagom—not too little and not too much.

chapter 2

lagom and happiness

A saying in Swedish, *Lagom är bäst*,
translates roughly as "The right amount is best."

scandi happiness

Sweden frequently comes in the top ten of the Happiness Report, a landmark global survey carried out by the UN each year. In fact, all the Scandinavian countries usually end up in the top part of the table. What is it about these countries that makes them score so highly, and so consistently, in these types of reports?

Sweden is often described as the ultimate model, where things are done right — gender equality, social security, and quality of life lead to happiness. Even though Swedish society has changed a lot in the past decade, as has

society in most other countries, Sweden still feels like a country with a culture that is geared toward people, and putting people first comes from a lagom attitude — achieving the balance between working hard and having time for the rest of your community and family. But you don't have to live in Sweden to practice lagom and boost your happiness and contentment. Lagom is more of a philosophy than a lifestyle, a central approach to life that says everyone can have a piece of the pie — and exactly the right piece — just in a lagom amount. It's a kind of Swedish Goldilocks approach, with everything "just right."

lagom is best

It turns out that our brains like things to be just right, too. The prefrontal cortex, which is in charge of planning ahead, making complex decisions, organizing, and multitasking, has the Goldilocks approach. Things have to be just right for it to function optimally. Amy Arnsten, a professor in neurobiology and psychology at Yale, who coined the Goldilocks comparison, suggests that both too little engagement and too much stress take us to the same ineffective place, so in order to perform at our best, we need to have balance.

A 2016 study, carried out by researchers in Hong Kong and Bulgaria, suggests that genetics can be key to happiness — so it could be in your DNA. The researchers found that populations with a high prevalence of a specific gene correlate to higher levels of perceived happiness in that country. This gene is responsible for sensory pleasure and pain reduction, which could explain the difference in happiness levels between European countries. Northern Europeans, and Swedes in particular, score highly on the happiness index and those populations carry high levels of the gene. The researchers do point out, though, that genetics is not the only determinant to happiness. A stable society, economically and politically, contributes, too.

DNA aside — and of course happiness isn't dependent on whether you have Scandi genes or not — this level of happiness could be explained quite simply with lagom, the concept that happiness can be found in having a life that is just so, not too much but not too little, and a sense that things are sufficiently good the way they are.

Most Swedes rely on the fact that the State will take care of them from cradle to grave, and the knowledge that they will not have to fight to survive fosters a sense of contentment. This means that Swedes have time to do things that are meaningful and add value to their lives. When you fill your life with meaning, you automatically find a sense of purpose and worth, which equals happiness. Live with the lagom approach and you will soon agree that life is pretty good the way it is; it could be better but it's fine the way it is, basically just right.

On my visits to Sweden, I am often struck by an aura of quiet contentment as if Swedes know they are on to something good, living life just the way they want and assuming that their way of doing things is a really excellent way. Often I have to admit, sometimes begrudgingly, that "yes, that is a rather clever way of organizing your kitchen cupboards." There must be something very comforting about knowing you are living life in just the right way.

lagom and contentment

If you live in a lagom way, contentment will surely follow, while striving for happiness can be counterproductive. Happiness studies, or positive psychology, is a relatively new area of research. In 1998, the American Psychological Association's newly appointed president, Dr Martin S. Seligman, in his first speech, launched this new branch of psychology. Happiness was going to be documented, measured, and controlled through techniques and interventions.

All of a sudden, happiness was something that could be packaged and sold for profit, and we were bombarded with books on "how to be happy" from both self-appointed happiness gurus and positive-psychologist academics. We had books, lectures, apps, and tools to teach us how to be happy and emphasize how happiness was not down to individual circumstances but could be manipulated and altered through various means and methods.

As it turned out, actively seeking happiness was actually making us more miserable. The happier you try to be, the less happy you end up being. If you

have a preformed idea of what happiness should feel like, there is a big chance that when something good actually happens, not only do you not feel as happy as expected, but you may also feel disappointed.

A study done in Berkeley, California, found that people who prioritized happiness felt lonelier on a

daily basis than those who didn't concentrate on it, as assessed through diary entries made over two weeks. In contrast, trying to find meaning in your life appears to be one way of creating a deeper and lasting feeling of wellbeing.

Philosophy has long recognized happiness and meaningfulness as two forms of wellbeing. In her book *The Power of Meaning*, Emily Esfhani Smith explores the writings of teachers such as Aristotle and authors such as Tolstoy, as well as recent research papers on meaningfulness. She found that the main attributes of a meaningful life are connecting and contributing to something other than yourself. This could be your family, your work, volunteering in the community, following outdoor pursuits, or religion. After giving birth to my first child, Alvar,

I remember thinking what a relief it was not to be so preoccupied with thinking about self-oriented goals and how I felt in every moment. Having someone else to feed and nurture gave me a real sense of contentment that I hadn't felt before. It's a cliché but I started to appreciate the smaller things in life. It gave me more of a sense of purpose in everything I did.

Lagom is a concept behind Swedish living in general and is very much engrained in the culture. As a consequence, it can be a bit tricky for an outsider to appreciate its value, the idea that lagom permeates everything you do, and how it links in to feelings of contentment and balance, a kind of sustainable positive outlook on life that feels natural. More of everything is not necessarily better and by using the lagom approach to many situations, that might become more obvious. A lagom mindset of "good enough" fosters an enduring kind of happiness. Of course, it is important to keep in mind that one person's "good enough" may be different from someone else's.

sharing the pot...

Central to Scandinavian culture is the idea of the shared pot where everyone contributes and everyone benefits. This allows us to enjoy life, knowing that the things we value, such as good medical care, are taken care of. When you don't have to worry about the basic needs in life, you have more time to devote to finding things that add meaning, such as spending time with your family, having a good work/life balance, and time to pursue an interest on the side. This is why you won't hear many Swedes grumble about paying high taxes; we know that this is what helps us to live a better life. Subsidized childcare allows parents to have a career. My friend Klara says that "everyone realizes that the whole of society gains when both parents are able to carry on working, so you don't lose talent in the workplace, especially women. Society needs children."

A lagom approach to working life not only allows people to take regular breaks throughout the day (known as fika—a kind of time out with cookies, see Chapter 3) but also to leave work at a decent time, and Sweden still seems to be efficient. It makes you wonder why all countries don't adopt the lagom approach to work.

Even though you are probably not able to relocate to Sweden and partake in the generous social care and time off, there are things that you can do to introduce a "good enough" concept to your own life. A lagom approach could lead to feelings of contentment just by

giving you the time to participate in things you love to do, be it playing music, gardening, or anything else. Having time to do these things adds value to your life. A big party is not necessary for happiness but having a hot drink with a friend could do it. Taking a walk in the park at lunchtime and noticing how warm the sun feels on your face, or planting seeds to grow on your windowsill, are lagom enough to give you feelings of contentment.

salad in a tub

One of the highlights of summer is being able to pick fresh salad daily, and you really don't need much space. Salad plants are fine for growing in a container. Position it in a convenient spot and enjoy the benefits of home-grown food.

You will need

galvanized metal tub

drainage crocks

pea gravel

potting mix

bendy twigs (optional)

salad plants of your choice e.g. arugula/ rocket, cut-and-come-again lettuce, sorrel. An edible flower, such as viola, adds a splash of color

Make holes in the bottom of the tub if you need to. Place a few crocks over the holes to help with drainage.

Add a layer of pea gravel to the bottom of the tub before filling with some potting mix until it nearly reaches the rim.

If you like, make a little twiggy fence to sit around the perimeter of the tub. Cut your twigs into lengths of about 16 inches/40cm Bend one into an arch and push it firmly into the potting mix. Continue like this, overlapping the arches to make a neat edging to the tub.

Scoop out a little of the potting mix and push in your plants, firming around each one as you go to keep them in place.

Space the plants about 1 inch/2.5cm apart, or cram in as many as possible if you want to pick the leaves when they're small and especially tasty. Keep the potting mix moist, watering throughout the growing season, and pick the leaves regularly to prevent the plants running to seed.

... and sharing the plot

Perennial flowers and shrubs, and berry bushes that carry on fruiting with a bit of love and care, are perpetual gifts that keep on giving. The happiness found in the lagom approach is not about hedonistic pleasures and squeezing the maximum benefits out of every situation. Planting a garden is a way of producing tangible results perhaps at a time when we might struggle to find meaning in our day-to-day life.

During a particular tumultuous time in my own life, when balance and a sense of rootedness were nowhere to be found, I signed up for an allotment/community garden and it was the best thing I could have done. In one go, so much was added to my life, rather than exhausting and draining me of my resources. I could have a quiet time without feeling as if I wasn't doing anything useful, and I had the company of the other gardeners while we were all tending our plots. Although we were working side by side we were not necessarily conversing, but it was a comforting thought that we were all there for the same purpose.

More often than not I would seek advice from Stan, Nigel, Tepa, and all the other green-fingered gurus who had been growing fruit and veg for longer than I had been in London. Looking back, I realize that the activity brought an enduring sense of contentment to my life and this is where my interest in growing your own began. It wasn't the attraction of showing off fine home-grown tomatoes (showing off is so un-lagom) but the sense that things were good just the way they were when I had my plot to balance up my otherwise very hectic life. The

The continuous cycle of planting and harvesting will give you a feeling that all's right with the world.

mindful activities of preparing the soil, weeding, and sowing seeds, the small banter about the best way to plant your courgettes, and of course having a sit down for the quintessential fika in the sun after doing some manual labor don't sound very rock'n'roll, but the pleasure in them can all be traced back to the idea of lagom. The foundations of lagom are essentially contentment, balance, and moderation in everything that you do, and the belief that if you take just enough from life for yourself, not too much, there will be enough for others to be happy, too.

ON THE LAGOM WAVELENGTH

The lagom approach can be applied to family living and many of your relationships. Swedes are known for their dislike of general conflict and any kind of emotional outburst—that would not be classified as lagom. Colin Moon, a communications expert from the UK who lives in Stockholm, comments that "Swedes rarely say yes or no. This means that instead of saying *ja* or *nej* they say *nja*, which means 'yes-but-no-but-yes-but.' You see, saying yes or no can lead to conflict, so Swedes avoid these words and replace them with 'it depends,' 'maybe,' and 'I'll see what I can do.'" By avoiding conflict, lagom is preserved for all and they just hope that the other person is on the same wavelength. Most Swedes will be.

the lagom way...
how to find your happiness

- Ask yourself "Is this good enough?" instead of "Can I do better?" Question if you are feeling content rather than asking if you are feeling happy. Even though the two aren't mutually exclusive, focusing on happiness only could lead to disappointment.

- Plant some seeds, nurture them, and watch them grow to give you a lasting sense of purpose. "Gardener's Delight" is an easy cherry tomato that you can grow either indoors or out. French radishes are usually foolproof and give you an early spring harvest. For flowers, not much can beat Nicotiana. Easy to grow, it has the most amazing scent from flowers that open at dusk. There are several varieties.

- Make time for those things that help you to feel balanced instead of worrying about what you think you should be doing to make you happier. Activities such as baking, making something decorative for the house, or getting outdoors more regularly could be the answer.

- Join a charitable organization to support a valuable cause. So for example, why not volunteer to help at tea parties for elderly people who may live on their own, and bring along some homemade cookies?

chapter 3

lagom and time

A sensible work/life balance, including plenty
of down time, leads to more contentment
and harmony.

take time out

Let's imagine a day at work in Sweden. You have been at work for about an hour and a half, you're ploughing through your emails, getting on with work, you've done some staring out of the window, getting on with more work, and then Anders taps you on the shoulder and tells you it's "fika time." You look at your watch, wondering if it's perhaps already lunchtime, and realize it's only 10 a.m. and you still haven't replied to Berit in accounts about why the invoices were late again. You know there is no getting out of it so you get up and walk into the fika room (yes, many offices have a dedicated space for this), and sit down with the rest of the staff. You have one cup of coffee, then perhaps *påtår* (which is just a word for the second cup of coffee. Third cup is called? Yes, correct. *Tretår*. Tre as in three.) You may also have a small cookie or a sandwich if you are feeling peckish (after all, you had breakfast at home very early in order to get to work by 8.30 a.m.).

After about 20 minutes or so you carry on with your work until 12.30 p.m. when you go out for lunch with some of your colleagues, including Solveig, who looks after reception and also the phones. She puts the answerphone on as the office is now closed for lunch and people will just have to call back. Then, an hour later, energized by food and a proper break, you tick off a lot of your to-do list until 3 p.m. when it's fika time again and you sit down to chat with your colleagues about anything not to do with work. This is not a strategy for multitasking. You may discuss the best way to eliminate killer slugs from the

garden or your local grocery store's offer on real butter but you don't talk about work because this is your break. Work talk is for work time. This is fika time. You realize by 4.52 p.m. that you still haven't replied to Berit so you send a quick message to her before logging out at 4.58 p.m. and heading home. All your colleagues are doing the same.

Sounds like the sort of day we would all like to have in the office, right? This is not dissimilar to what my English friend Tim experienced when he was working in Sweden — numerous interruptions to share a hot drink with your colleagues. Of course, not every office operates in this way. Some people might have their coffee on the go or sit in front of the computer while they eat their lunch. But it's not too far from the truth for many Swedes. The fact is that fika time has now become a pretty established concept and has become a way to define *any* switch-off moment, when you step away from a busy and hectic world.

After *tack* (thank you, and also please) and *hej* (hello), fika is the next word to learn. Gathering for coffee and something sweet to eat is something we do every day, several times a day, with friends, family, or colleagues. If someone suggests a meet-up for fika, you know what it means — the perfect lagom kind of get together. You know it won't take up too much of your time but will be long enough to talk about the main things on your mind, which can be anything from family events to work-related issues (but not in the office). Anything not covered you can talk about next time.

Fika time is not complicated. All you need is coffee and cookies, either home-made or from a packet. Most Swedish recipes adopt the lagom approach, balancing difficulty and ease — not too hard, not too simple, ingredients all in one bowl, using measuring spoons. The scales come out for something uneven, such as berries, but you can always take an *ögonmått* (basically, measurement by eye).

The importance of fika lies in having a break
and being together.

Try this...

äppelbröd *apple bread with cardamom*

My childhood home had several apple trees in the garden and my parents would store the apples throughout winter, each one wrapped in layers of newspaper. My dad, Arne, was a bit of an expert when it came to grafting different varieties onto the trees, so several of the trees bore different kinds of apples. My mom, Brita, often makes this apple bread and it's one of the apple recipes I love the best. The combination of cardamom, tart apples, and sweet dough is just heavenly. Mom thinks the recipe may have originated from a newspaper back in the '80s, but she has made it her own now.

Makes 2

2 oz/50 g fresh yeast or 1 oz/25 g active dry yeast

⅔ cup/150 g butter, plus extra for greasing

2 cups plus 2 tablespoons/500 ml whole/full-fat milk

scant ½ cup/90 g superfine/caster sugar

1 teaspoon ground cardamom

1 egg

5¾ cups/770 g all-purpose/plain flour, plus extra for dusting

beaten egg, to glaze

Filling

6–8 apples (cooking apples work well)

1 tablespoon ground cardamom

½ cup/100 g sugar

¾ cup/100 g raisins or other dried fruit (chopped dried apricots work well)

juice of 1 lemon

Grease 2 baking sheets and line with parchment paper.

If using fresh yeast, crumble it into a bowl. Melt the butter in a pan over a gentle heat, add the milk, and heat to finger temperature (36–37°C/97–98°F). Pour the mixture over the yeast and blend until dissolved. Add the sugar, cardamom, and egg. If using active dry yeast, mix this with the flour. Add the flour to the bowl. Keep mixing until you have a pliable, smooth dough that is starting to come away from the sides of the bowl. Cover with a cloth and let the dough prove in a warm place for about 30 minutes (or until doubled in size).

Meanwhile, make the apple filling. Peel and core the apples. Cut them into thin wedges, and mix them with cardamom, sugar and raisins in a bowl. I also like to squeeze some fresh lemon juice on top to stop them from browning.

Turn the dough out on to a lightly floured work surface. Knead it, then divide into four equal pieces and shape into balls. Roll the balls out into circles about 10 inches/25 cm in diameter and place two of them on the baking sheets. Divide the apple mixture equally between the two, spreading it over the dough but leaving a gap of about 2 inches/5 cm around the edge. Place the other two dough circles on top of the filling, and pinch the edges of the dough together so the filling doesn't leak out. Make a cross on the top so some air can escape. Leave to rise for a further 30 minutes.

Preheat the oven to 200°C/400°F/Gas 6.

When ready to bake, brush lightly with beaten egg, then bake in the preheated oven for 20–30 minutes until golden brown. Transfer from the baking sheets to a wire rack, and cover with a clean dish towel while they cool.

Try this... brysselkex *Brussels biscuits*

In 1945 the book *Sju Sorters Kakor* was published in Sweden. The title—*Seven Kinds of Biscuits*—referred to the number of different types of cookies a hostess was expected to serve to her guests. Too many and she was showing off, too few and she was being mean. Seven kinds were just lagom. Brysselkex were one of the original seven. My mom makes these every Christmas and rolls them in sugar that she has colored red. You can vary the colors according to the season—try green for spring, yellow for Easter, or a mix of blue, yellow, and red for a Superman birthday party!

Makes about 50

Dough

¾ cup plus 2 tablespoons/200 g butter, plus extra for greasing

2¼ cups/300 g all-purpose/plain flour

7 tablespoons/85 g caster sugar

1 tablespoon vanilla sugar or vanilla extract

Decoration

½ cup/100 g granulated sugar

a few drops of food coloring

Start with the decoration. Mix the sugar and food coloring together in a plastic bag so the sugar is evenly colored.

Mix the butter, flour, sugar, and vanilla sugar or extract together in a bowl to make a smooth, even dough. Divide the dough into two, and shape each piece into a sausage 1¼ –1½ inches/3–4 cm in diameter. Sprinkle the colored sugar on a flat plate and roll each piece of dough in it, until it is coated all around. Place in the fridge to chill for 30 minutes.

Preheat the oven to 175°C/350°F/Gas 4. Grease 3 or 4 baking sheets and line with parchment paper.

Using a sharp knife, cut the dough into slices ¼ inch/5 mm thick and arrange on the baking sheets. Bake in the preheated oven for about 10 minutes. Watch them carefully as the sugar on the edges can burn if baked for too long. Transfer to wire racks to cool.

Try this...

nötchokladrutor *chocolate and nut squares*

When my parents had gatherings at home with friends or family, after dessert there always had to be a *kaka till kaffet*, which basically means a "biscuit with coffee." When coffee was served, you also wanted something a little bit sweet to go with it, so my mom would often bake these. They are quick to make, the perfect lagom size, and my favorite from the cookie tray. I particularly love the crunch of the hazelnuts on top.

Makes about 20 squares

7 tablespoons/100 g butter, at room temperature, plus extra for greasing

scant ¾ cup/140 g superfine/caster sugar

½ teaspoon baking powder

2 tablespoons cocoa powder

1 egg

1 teaspoon vanilla sugar or vanilla extract

½ cup plus 1 tablespoon/75 g all-purpose/plain flour

¾ cup/100 g chopped hazelnuts

Preheat the oven to 200°C/400°F/Gas 6. Grease a baking sheet about 10 x 14 inches/25 x 35 cm or larger, and line with parchment paper. If using a larger baking sheet, only prepare an area no larger than 10 x 14 inches/25 x 35 cm.

Cream the butter and sugar together until pale and fluffy, using a hand-held electric whisk or a balloon whisk. Add the baking powder and cocoa and blend until smooth. Add the egg and vanilla sugar or extract and whisk until incorporated. Sift in the flour and mix until blended and you have a batter that resembles smooth butter. Spread the batter evenly on the baking sheet. Scatter the chopped nuts on top.

Bake in the preheated oven for 15 minutes and cut into squares while still warm. Let cool and store in an airtight container.

Try this...

faster barbro's tekakor *Aunt Barbro's teacakes*

My dad's older sister, Barbro, is legendary when it comes to cooking. She no longer hosts the big family gatherings that she once used to as she is now 93 years old, but all of us cousins—and there are lots of us—have memories of sitting in her warm kitchen that was fragrant with the scents of home cooking and coffee. We ate these teacakes with cheese and drank home-made blackcurrant cordial. My kids are no different—they love them too.

Makes about 25

¾ cup/75 g rolled/porridge oats

1⅛ cup/150 g linseeds

1¼ cups/300 ml whole/full-fat milk

2 oz/50 g fresh yeast or 1 oz/25 g active dry yeast

2 teaspoons salt

3 tablespoons corn syrup/golden syrup

1 scant cup/200 ml crème fraîche or natural yogurt

3¾ cups/500 g wheatmeal flour

1¼ cups/170 g wholewheat/wholemeal flour

1 teaspoon baking powder

butter, for greasing

Place the oats and linseeds in a pan with 1 scant cup/200 ml water. Cook gently for 5 minutes until the mixture has a porridge consistency (you may need to add a little more water if the mixture is too dry). Add 1 scant cup/200 ml of the milk and let the mixture cool.

Heat the remaining milk to about 36–37°C/97–98°F. If using fresh yeast, mix it with the hot milk until dissolved. If using active dry yeast, pour the heated milk in a bowl and sprinkle the active dry yeast on top, cover, and leave to activate and become frothy and bubbly.

Add the salt and corn/golden syrup to the bowl of milk and yeast. Stir in the cooled oat, linseed and water mixture, mix well, and add the crème fraîche or yogurt. Add

both the flours and the baking powder and mix either by hand or in a food mixer fitted with a dough hook until it forms a dough (it's ok if it's a bit sticky). Leave to prove in a warm place for about an hour or until doubled in size.

Grease and line a baking sheet with parchment paper.

Punch down/knock back the dough, knead it again to make a smooth dough, and then cut into two pieces. Roll out each piece of dough to about ½ inch/1 cm thick and cut round shapes using a cup 3¼–4 inches/8–10 cm in diameter (I find that my Moomin cup is the perfect size for cutting lagom-size teacakes!). Prick the circles lightly on top with a fork and place on a baking sheet. Carry on cutting shapes until no dough remains (any offcuts can be rolled out to cut more teacakes). Leave to prove for about 30 minutes.

Preheat the oven to 225°C/430°F/Gas 7. Dust the tops of the teacakes with flour and bake in the middle of the oven for about 13 minutes until golden brown. Cool on a wire rack, covered with a clean dish towel.

To serve, slice in half and serve with butter and cheese, topped with slices of cucumber or red bell pepper if you wish. Or for a true Swedish touch, add a dollop of orange marmalade on top of the cheese.

These teacakes freeze well. Once defrosted, eat within a day or so.

rulltårta
rolled cake

This is the Scandinavian version of a roly-poly. It's super quick to do and you can make it a bit more elaborate by popping a dollop of whipped cream on top with some berries for a garnish and calling it a fancy cake. The sponge is very light and can happily take any fillings you care to add, such as cream and berries as shown here, preserves/jam, or my personal favorite—homemade, smooth-with-no-lumps apple sauce. If using preserves/jam or apple sauce for the filling, you will need about 1 cup/300 g.

Makes 20 slices

butter, for greasing

3 eggs

⅔ cup minus 1 tablespoon/120 g superfine/caster sugar, plus extra for sprinkling

2 tablespoons milk

⅔ cup/90 g all-purpose/plain flour

1 teaspoon baking powder

¼ cup/30 g potato starch or cornstarch/cornflour

½ cup/100 ml heavy/double cream

2 cups/250 g raspberries

Preheat the oven to 250°C/475°F/Gas 9. Do this in good time so the oven is very hot when the batter is ready. Grease and line a 12 x 16 inch/30 x 40 cm baking sheet with parchment paper.

Whisk the eggs and sugar together until pale and fluffy. Stir in the milk. Mix the flour, baking powder, and potato starch or cornstarch/cornflour together and fold gently into the egg mixture. The batter will be a bit stiffer than a regular sponge mixture.

Spread the batter on to the parchment paper, filling the baking sheet, and bake in the preheated oven for 5 minutes.

Cut another piece of parchment paper to the same size as the baking sheet and sprinkle sugar over it. When the cake comes out of the oven, gently tip it out onto the sugar-coated paper with the top of the cake facing down. Peel off the paper from the base of the cake (if the paper is tricky to remove, try brushing it with a little cold water to help release it).

To make the filling, whip the cream until thick and holding its shape. Mix the whipped cream and raspberries together, mashing the raspberries slightly so the cream turns pink. Spread on top of the cake while it is still warm and gently roll it up, peeling back the sugared paper as you go so that it doesn't end up inside the rolled cake. (If you roll the cake while it is warm, the sponge won't crack as much.) Keep the cake rolled up in paper and stored in the fridge until you are ready to serve, to prevent it drying out and to make it easier to slice.

lagom — work/life balance

A better work/life balance is one thing that many Swedes who return home after working abroad comment on. They find that life is less hectic because they have more time for activities not related to work. It's a curious thing and one wonders how this works since everyone has the same 24 hours in the day. Well, it has a lot to do with the lagom mentality. Jessica, an ex-pat from London explains, "I think work/life balance [in Sweden] is much better, because you work lagom before you take your fika and your lunch break."

However, even though for most people the lagom practice of taking regular fika breaks as a team is a wonderful thing, when you want something done, it can be an issue.

Frances, an American living in Sweden, told me of the frustration when you pop into the surgery to get your blood test done and no one is there to do it because they are all having their break. Together. At the same time. Crystal from the UK tells how she took her car to the garage for an MOT and they wouldn't accept it because they were having their morning fika. It was 9.15 a.m.

Non-Swedes tend to agree that once you get used to it, you accept it as something positive. You just learn to know when it's not a good time to get your car serviced or your blood test done and so avoid the times when people are probably having a fika break or lunch break, and not after 5 p.m. of course.

Flexitime is very common in Sweden and encouraged by employers. Also, after having children you have a legal right to reduce your hours to 25 percent.

Beside getting five weeks' annual vacation, Swedes also have a fair

share of public holidays, or red days as they like to call them (because they are marked in red on the calendar). Red days add up to about two weeks' extra time off. If you're lucky, your employer may give you an extra half day before the red day, just to get you in the mood, and if a red day falls on a Thursday, the company may give you a *klämdag*, which basically means a squeezed day, the

LAGOM FLEXITIME

Colin Moon, an English communications expert who lives in Stockholm, comments that "most Swedes are dedicated to finding a healthy work/life balance. They might say they work hard; it's just that they are not often there. When they are at work, they are very effective — but not before 8.30 as they make use of their flexitime, and not after 16.00 because they have to pick up the kids from preschool, and not after 14.00 on Fridays if you don't mind."

one in between the red day and the weekend. That day might as well not exist on the work calendar. An American website on how to do business in Sweden advises that foreign partners should not expect to meet their Swedish counterparts after 4 p.m. on weekdays since 5 p.m. is going home time, and not to schedule meetings in June, July, or August or late February through March because these are popular times to go on vacation.

You do have to wonder how Swedes actually get any work done. The thing is, we Swedes really value that work/life balance, and work hard to achieve it. At work, and in many situations in life, we focus on what has to be done rather than doing unnecessary things that can eat into our leisure time.

Who wouldn't want to live somewhere where time is so valued by the government? Who wouldn't want 480 days out for parental leave, to be taken before the child is eight years old? You are even entitled to time off to be with sick children. *Vabba*, as it's called, is not a word for which you will find an English equivalent.

reclaim your time

A lagom approach to time is really about reclaiming your own time. Log out from your computer to leave the office on time. Don't have email or social-media notifications on your phone, and switch it off when you are with your family (if your kids will let you, that is). Set specific work hours and ignore your email outside of those hours. You will probably find that you are just as efficient as before. Boasting about working an 80-hour week is definitely not lagom; knowing that there's a time to work and a time not to work is lagom. Working overtime is neither valued nor seen as necessary. In fact, it can be seen as an indication of poor planning and time management.

Working too much and not taking time off for whatever you want to do eventually creates a feeling of mistrust and can cause a lack of motivation and an ebbing away of loyalty toward your employer. This is where the lagom way fits in perfectly. It means you work enough to get your tasks done but not too much, so you don't miss out on rest, recharging, and having fun. A pretty simple approach, but one that we quite often don't feel we are able to choose.

While it's all very well hearing about the Swedish system, how can you achieve a decent work/life balance when you don't have five weeks' vacation, or more red days than the average American has in annual leave, or even *vabba*? You might think that you are not able to change anything about an office culture in which we are encouraged to work long hours.

However, think about the time that you do have that is just your own, and

start by reclaiming more of that. Too often we spend our free time doing things that actually we don't really want to do. For example, a typical Saturday may be spent ferrying children around to various activities when sometimes neither you nor they are that keen on them. For some reason, we are often caught up in thinking that this is what we should be doing. How would your weekend look if you didn't have these activities?

If you had a lagom approach to time and balance, what would you do? Well, not rush out of bed on a Saturday morning to stand around a windy tennis court, or scramble around for a karate kit that's been in the laundry basket since last weekend. We all have duties and things that need to be taken care of at the weekend, that's unavoidable, but perhaps try to scale down the number of outside activities and include real family time instead. Ask yourself if the week and weekend ahead is really lagom work/life/family balanced and see what your gut instinct tells you. Of course, some people and kids thrive on plenty of things to do but then that is lagom for them. However, most people need quite a bit of uninterrupted time in order to wind down and find balance.

Your non-working hours should be for home, family, self-care, and relaxation.

HOME SWEET HOME

As non-Swedes will attest, we Swedes have a tendency to keep private and professional lives separate and this can feel a tad unwelcoming at first, but it can be explained as being because Swedes value their leisure time so much. Lagom time is really spent at home, not reached for on the outside. Home is where everyone can feel relaxed and can recharge their batteries. It's where lagom can flourish.

the lagom way...
how to find your lagom time

꙳ Reduce the amount of activities you plan during the week and weekend. Try to leave one day free per weekend. That is when you can find your lagom time and allow yourself to be spontaneous and spend quality time with your family.

꙳ If you can't leave the office at 5.30, try leaving a little earlier than you usually do to see how that affects your day. If you know that you have to leave at a fixed time, you will be more efficient.

꙳ Being well rested is also key to being efficient and experiencing fewer feelings of stress. Try to go to bed in good time and get up a little earlier than usual. Having an extra 30 minutes in the morning instead of rushing can give you a feeling of owning more of your day—a small gesture of self-empowerment. If it's still dark, make the extra time special by lighting a candle and having tea in a favorite mug.

꙳ Ask yourself if your week is looking lagom in terms of activities and commitments. Perhaps you could arrange your social life differently. A book club is a good example of a lagom activity. You meet friends, enjoy socializing at someone's house, and you also have to spend time reading. Taking a walk, perhaps in nature, is a perfectly harmonious way to spend lagom time, especially if you bring fika along.

chapter 4

lagom and food

When cooking focuses on simplicity and
nourishment, people feel encouraged to
start cooking again.

seasonal and local

Sweden, the country of lagom, isn't known for having a food culture with knock-out flavors. What we do have, however, are fantastic raw ingredients and genuine food traditions. At Christmas, for example, we take food intake to excess and lagom goes out of the window. It's non-stop eating, including many traditional offerings that must somehow be consumed at some point, and at this time of year the tills at the state-controlled liquor store, Systembolaget, keep on ringing.

The approach to food in Sweden focuses on seasonal and local. We love to forage, which combines two of our favorite things — spending time outdoors and eating. A common pastime is to get a bucket, load some fika into a backpack, and go out into the forest to pick berries and mushrooms. Most Swedes know how to make some classic foraging recipes, such as berry crumbles and nettle soup. I have many memories of this from childhood, including being out and about picking lingonberries and blueberries, and trudging after my dad searching for mushrooms in the darker and denser parts of the forest, where the sunlight struggled to penetrate and where the forest floor was mostly dried-up pine needles. That is where you could find the "gold of the forest" — chantarelles. I imagine I was probably complaining about wet socks or that my bucket was heavy, but then you saw them, gleaming like pieces of gold, almost hidden by a mossy rock. It was worth it then because you knew the reward would be sautéed buttered mushrooms that tasted of the forest and autumn rain.

According to a 2016 report from Food & Friends (a Swedish communications bureau), four out of every five Swedes say they are interested in cooking, but 62 percent of all recipes cooked are the same 10 recipes. A vegetarian choice made it to number 8, which is perhaps a sign that we are now more focused on health and environment. Our food needs to leave a good taste, not only in our mouths but also in our minds.

food produced the lagom way

In Sweden, one of the buzzwords is *klimatsmart*, which basically means "smart eating for the climate," or in other words considering the environment when choosing your ingredients. This has become very trendy in Sweden.

Marie Lönneskog Hogstadius, business developer at the Federation of Swedish Farmers, explains that "Swedish people think it's lagom to contribute their bit for the climate by shopping for Swedish meat, because our way of producing meat is responsible. For example, farmers use the lowest level of antibiotics in Europe and they keep the cattle grazing outside. That in turn contributes to keeping our landscape open and living. It's not complicated. It's an easy choice. It's just lagom."

However, questions such as "Is this product organic/environmental/fair trade?" or "Is the meat grass fed?" or "Is it gluten free?" are sometimes difficult to answer. If you start to feel that this is the only way to feed your family, it can become exhausting and not lagom at all. Even though considering the environment may be a priority for mankind, in all honesty, do we really want to think about it all the time? Sometimes you can be too lagom about lagom. I got frustrated recently about being unable to recycle all my plastic in the weekly collection. I decided to keep it in my car instead, ready to be taken to the local recycling center when I had a free moment, which I rarely did. Eventually, it became too much to think about and, in the end, I just threw it out with the rest of the trash and made a choice about where my lagom was.

KEEP IT LAGOM

When you have top ingredients, you don't need to do much to them, which may explain the flavors of the Scandinavian kitchen. Karin Mörk, a forest engineer, says that "lagom is often used to describe how we flavor our food — it should be just lagom. Typical Swedish flavors are quite mild — salt, pepper, aniseed, herbs such as dill and parsley, and cardamom, vanilla, a blend of sweet and sour — but often we just let the flavor of the raw material shine, so to speak."

Legendary Swedish cookery writer Anna Bergenström, who has sold more than one million cookery books in Scandinavia alone, says she "... loves the word lagom. It's a word we should be happy to have in our vocabulary. It says so much without having to explain a whole lot."

waste not, want not

Research done by the Swedish Environmental Protection Agency claimed that 70 percent of all food waste happens at home, and I don't suppose it's much better elsewhere. On the other hand, every fourth Swede wants to take a lunchbox to work more often than they do now. I can't help but think there is a contradiction here, a gap that we should be able to bridge. Food is so readily available we don't worry about chucking out a few wilted veggies or sad-looking mushrooms. Perhaps if we could be a bit more mindful about where it comes from, we would realize the impact that growing and transporting it has on the environment, and then feel respect for the person who put the effort into growing it and cooking it, even if that person happens to be you.

I grew up on a farm and most of our food was local, by which I mean fruit from the garden, potatoes and carrots from the field opposite to see us through the winter, preserve made from berries found in the forest, milk from our cows, and ham from a pig reared by my father. To throw food away was classed almost as a sin and certainly disrespectful. Perhaps my upbringing was the stuff of foodie fairy tales, but we can all consider a meal as something to treasure and a way of spending time together.

Lagom cooking means making a meal that feeds all of you at the table and doesn't require much effort, just enough to show you care—pressing a button on the microwave doesn't do it. Instead, try to source good ingredients so your food will taste good with minimum preparation, plan your meals, and batch cook.

When you think about food shopping and meal planning, also consider your other commitments during the week and save longer cooking sessions for the weekend when you have time. Set up a planner in your kitchen where you can add all the activities throughout the week, and think about how much time you have to cook each day, and what snacks you need. This will help you to save money and cut food waste.

GOOD INGREDIENTS

Being frugal and working with simple ingredients to save money and time is nothing new. *Kajsa's kokbok*, a classic Swedish cookbook from 1937, talked about not wasting food, saving your pennies, meal planning, and the importance of simple but good ingredients. The motivation might have been scarcity but the sentiment hasn't changed. The book also notes the importance of freshness of food, for example, the difference in taste between a fish caught the day before and one not so fresh i.e. caught two days before.

Try eating with the seasons — good for the environment, your bank balance, and your body, too. Buy in bulk and freeze, pickle, or make preserves. Seville orange marmalade will give you sunshine in a jar all year. Eat it with cheese on crackerbread for the perfect Swedish snack.

Bear in mind that it's better to be sitting down together enjoying a meal than spending some of that time preparing a complicated recipe. Keep a few simple, good ingredients at hand, and a few basic recipes up your sleeve, to help minimize stress. Try growing some herbs — they will really add zing to your cooking. Basil, oregano, chives, and parsley are as happy on a sunny window sill as they are outside. Just make sure to cut them before they bloom for more flavor.

If you learn how to cook lagom,
you will waste less.

just enough knowledge

Of course, Sweden is not immune to faddy food trends and fast-food restaurants. Problems with obesity are discussed in the media constantly. However, interest in simple cooking and basic skills is huge, as evidenced by the success of the book *Hemkunskap (Home Economics)* by Swedish Michelin star-studded chef Mathias Dahlgren. Spend lagom time in the kitchen only, he implies, i.e. not too much, but not too little, either.

He points out that we now know more about food than ever before but the basic skills are slowly disappearing, which can be confusing for the home cook (although kids are taught home economics up to the age of 16). We are bombarded with recipes from literally everywhere and ingredients from all corners of the world. The pressure is to be like a Michelin chef every night, and that is definitely not lagom. It can become totally overwhelming and add to feelings of inadequacy.

I think the key is to plan your week from the viewpoint of what your week actually looks like rather than how you would like it to look. Some evenings you just don't have time to cook. It's better to accept that than to have a bad conscience. Those busy days are when you want to have something stashed in

Ultimately, lagom is about moderation
and balance.

the fridge or freezer to heat up, or enough ingredients to make a straightforward meal. Maybe you have some eggs and some left-over rice and peas — that is enough for dinner. On such days, don't worry about having to consume all your nutrients every day. Stress has been shown to cause more issues with health than occasionally deficient diets. Our memories are usually of loving moments spent together. As my brother-in-law Birger once said, and I have applied it (in my mind) to many fraught and un-lagom moments, "At least we are together."

KEEP IT SIMPLE

Anna Bergenström, one of Sweden's best-loved cookery book authors, recalls that when her kids were young "... we ate a lot of soup, simple ones, sometimes with lentils but always with bread, because the important thing was that we sat down together so everyone had time to talk about their day." She explains that her goal "... is that everyone should be able to make my recipes even though they feel they can't cook."

take a break

You can't talk about lagom and food and not mention fika. You have *merienda* in Spain and afternoon tea in the UK but nowhere else in the world do you have a word that describes a moment of recharging and mindfulness in a way that everyone can understand — from five-year-old Ellen through Arne, a retired bank manager aged 90. Jennie Loveday from the UK, who works in *fritids* (after-school care), explains that at her work they take fika breaks at their discretion, while making sure that at least one staff member remains available for each age group, or they simply bring the fika to the room where the kids play. In this case, everyone wins — the staff get their break and the kids still have someone to look after them. A reminder that a fika break is a way to recharge and center yourself is Jennie's account of how at *fritids* they also call fika for children "... when they have spent more time out than in, or if we feel there is unexplained tension in the group. It acts like a reset button, bringing everyone together and having a few minutes of relaxation."

Yes, we all want ways to re-center in times of stress, especially if we can have coffee and a *kanelbulle* (cinnamon roll) to go along with it. Remember the Swedish mantra, "work lagom before fika and lunch." Repeat this to yourself during your next working day. Bring in some *kladdkaka* (sticky chocolate cake with a gooey center) and I am sure everyone will join you. Eventually. Once they realize that taking a break from working will actually make them more efficient.

SURRENDER TO FIKA

Autun Purser, a deep-sea biologist, came to enjoy the fika breaks when he worked for a time at the research station on Tjärnö, an island off the west coast of Sweden.

"Virtually the entire laboratory staff would meet, either in the modern canteen or outside on picnic benches, next to the delightful Kosterfjord, for this involved process of coffee consumption, cake eating, gossiping, and commiserating about the loss of some animal, experiment, or grant application. For many of us visitors, this was an enjoyable process, as was the similar afternoon stop. For others, especially those used to working in high-pressure, internally competitive institutes, this enforced break was a source of growing attrition."

fika to keep you going

You might wonder how healthy it is to stuff yourself with cookies and wash it down with gallons of coffee every day. Actually, it might be better for your health than you think to have regular small breaks with something to eat throughout the day. Research has found that a regular intake of glucose keeps your brain functioning much better, because even though the brain makes up 2 percent of body weight, it takes 20 percent of the body's energy. So just by thinking, using your eyes and ears, coping with stress, and trying to remember all the tasks you

have to get through, you are using a lot of energy. This research also linked low glucose levels to failures of self-control.[1] So, if you think about it, having that fika at 3 p.m. will help you to walk past the donut shop or clothes sale later, because a fika snack actually supports your brain in making the right choices.

In fact, there is something lagom about that—resisting impulsivity when you need to, frugality, regulating your emotions, saving money, and feeling quite good about it.

---

[1] "The Physiology of Willpower, linking blood glucose to Self-Control," Mattew T. Galliot, Roy F. Baumeister; *Personality and Social Psychology Review*, November 2007.

fläderblomssaft *elderflower cordial*

This is cordial like my mother used to make. Dilute it with soda or sparkling water to make a wonderfully refreshing drink or use it undiluted in cooking. Pick elderflowers in bloom and if you haven't got time to whip up some cordial, freeze the flowers and make it in the midst of winter. If you are going to freeze the cordial, you can reduce the sugar content.

Makes a generous 2 liters/2 quarts

25 elderflower heads

3 unwaxed lemons, scrubbed

3¼ lb/1.5 kg caster/superfine sugar

5 cups/1.2 liters boiling water

2 oz/55 g citric acid

Shake the elderflowers well to remove any insects (if you're going to freeze the flowers to use later, do this first!) Put the flowers into a clean bucket or large bowl and add the thinly sliced lemons.

In a pan, dissolve the sugar in the water over a low heat. Add the citric acid to make a smooth syrup, and carefully pour it over the elderflowers and lemons. Cover with a clean cloth and leave for 2–3 days.

Strain the cordial through a sieve lined with muslin/cheesecloth into a large jug/pitcher, and pour into sterilized bottles. Store the cordial in the refrigerator, or freeze in ziplock bags.

Try this... **nässelsoppa** *nettle soup*

I remember taking walks as a child with my older sister, Anna-Karin, collecting early nettle shoots to make this classic soup. It celebrates the arrival of spring as much as the chirping of returning birds, the flowering of wood anemones, and the budding of leaves. When picking nettles, select the first new shoots or the top shoots (about 4 inches/10cm from the top). Bigger nettles are more fiberous and don't taste as nice. Always pick nettles that are growing away from roads and wash them well. If you can't get nettles, this soup works well with spinach, too.

Serves 4

9 oz/250 g nettles

6¼ cups/1½ liters chicken or vegetable stock, or water

3 tablespoons butter

2 shallots, chopped

3 tablespoons all-purpose/plain flour

freshly grated nutmeg (optional)

sea salt and freshly ground black pepper

3½ tablespoons/50 ml heavy/double cream (optional)

chopped chives, to serve

Place the nettles in a bowl, cover with water and swirl around to rinse them well. Discard any thick stalks.

Drain the nettles, place them in a large pan, and cover with the stock or water. Bring to the boil and cook at a steady boil for 15 minutes. Drain the liquid and reserve, keeping it warm. Rinse the

nettles in cold water (a trick to keep their bright green color). Chop finely and set aside.

Melt the butter in a pan, add the shallots, and cook gently to soften them. Add the flour to the pan and stir to make a roux.

Add the warm reserved stock to the roux, stirring to avoid lumps forming, and cook for a few minutes. Add the chopped nettles and season with nutmeg, salt, and pepper. Add the cream, if using, and simmer for 10 minutes.

If you want a smooth soup, use a blender because a stick blender won't be powerful enough. Serve the soup with plenty of chopped chives.

For a more substantial meal, hard-cook/ boil or poach some eggs and serve these in the bowls of soup—their color contrasts well with the green of the nettles. You could also add a chopped potato at the same time as you add the nettles, to add bulk to the soup, but make sure the potato is cooked before blending the soup. Crumbled feta cheese, crispy bacon, or chopped smoked salmon also work well as additional toppings.

Try this... blåbärsoppa *blueberry soup*

I have many memories of drinking blueberry soup from a flask when out in nature, especially in winter time, so hot I always slightly burned my lips. It usually came from a packet and was whisked with hot water. It's great for a hike because it's filling, gives you energy, and warms you up. This recipe is perfect to make when berries are in season, although frozen ones work just as well. I like to add some lemon juice as the blueberries tend to be sweeter than the wild bilberries originally used and the added tartness of lemon brings the flavor closer to the real thing.

Serves 4

3¾ cups/500 g blueberries, fresh or frozen

4 tablespoons sugar

2 tablespoons potato starch

1 tablespoon fresh lemon juice

Place the blueberries in a pan with 2 cups plus 2 tablespoons/500 ml water and simmer for 5 minutes, then add the sugar and continue to cook until the sugar dissolves. Remove from the heat.

Mix the potato starch with 2 tablespoons cold water until the starch dissolves and mix slowly into the blueberries, stirring to avoid any lumps. Return the pan to the stove and heat it gently, but don't let it reach boiling point or the texture will become a bit gloopy. The soup should have the consistency of light/single cream—if you find it's too thick, add a bit more water or if it's too thin, add a few more blueberries. Add the lemon juice and remove from the heat.

Blend the soup with a stick mixer or in a blender. Serve hot or warm. Alternatively, chill the soup in the fridge before serving (it will keep for about a week in the fridge) and add on top of your porridge in the morning or pour over yogurt or ice cream.

Try this… smulpaj *summer fruit crumble*

This is something you could whip up quickly if you have unexpected guests. It's just on the fancy side of lagom for fika, but still lagom. Frozen berries (such as redcurrants, raspberries, blackcurrants, or blackberries) work really well with this, but apples or rhubarb are equally good. Aim for a double layer of fruit and a thin layer of topping.

Makes 4–5

1⅓ cups/180 g all-purpose/
plain flour (or a mixture of
1 cup minus 1½ tablespoons/
120 g flour and ⅔ cup/60 g
rolled/porridge oats)

½ teaspoon baking powder
(optional)

½ cup/100 g granulated or
superfine/caster sugar, plus
3 tablespoons for the fruit

½ cup plus 1 tablespoon/
125 g cold butter, plus extra
for greasing

1¾–3¾ cups/250–500 g
mixed berries (red or
blackcurrants, blackberries,
raspberries, strawberries,
pitted cherries), fresh or
frozen

Preheat the oven to 175°C/350°F/Gas 4. Grease a round ovenproof dish, 10 inches/25 cm in diameter.

In a bowl mix together the flour (or flour and oat mixture), baking powder, if using, sugar, and butter until it turns into small lumps. Try not to get them too small and avoid a breadcrumb texture as the topping needs to be chunky.

Mix the berries with 3 tablespoons sugar and place in the ovenproof dish. Cover with the flour and butter mixture and bake in the preheated oven for about 30 minutes. (You can prepare and cook this ahead if you wish, then reheat for 7–8 minutes.) Serve with vanilla ice cream or a dollop of whipped cream.

Try this…

jordgubbskräm *swedish berry dessert*

This is a dessert that can be eaten at any time of the day. When I was growing up, there was always a bowl of this in the fridge or on the stove. I loved eating it warm with cold milk poured over and some Swedish crackerbread crunched up on the top. My favorite flavor was cherry, mainly because the cherry tree in our garden produced fruit every other year only. Then again, I also loved strawberry and raspberry. Oh, and gooseberry too… I have recently rediscovered this recipe—now I often make it for my kids and I can't understand why I ever stopped making it. It's a dish that tastes of summer.

Serves 4

1¾ cups/250 g berries (strawberries, raspberries, blueberries, pitted cherries—either a mixture or just one kind)

½ cup/100 g granulated sugar

2 tablespoons potato starch

Place the berries in a pan with 1¾ cups/400 ml water and simmer over a gentle heat for 10 minutes. Lower the heat and add the sugar, then let it cook gently for a few more minutes until the sugar has dissolved. Remove from the heat.

Mix the potato starch with 4 tablespoons water and slowly add it to the berries, stirring to avoid any lumps forming.

Return the pan to the heat and bring it almost to boiling point, but don't let it boil—the texture should be like a thin jelly. Pour into a serving dish.

Serve warm with cold milk poured over. If not serving immediately, cover with a plate to avoid a crust forming on the top.

the lagom way...
how to be lagom about your food

- Use your freezer. Make sure you label packs so you don't get out a chili when you really want strawberries. Use your ice-cube tray to freeze herbs, cream, coconut milk. Freeze spotty old bananas to make ice cream or put in smoothies. Make elderflower cordial and freeze it in ziplock bags, which is a safe way to avoid it going off.

- Avoid sad and wilted veggies. Keep salad leaves and green leafy vegetables fresh for longer by washing them and keeping them in a sealed bag in the salad drawer of the fridge. Got an abundance of parsley? Chop it up and store it in a jar in the freezer for later use.

- Be climate smart with your food. Skip expensive ingredients imported from all over the world, which may never get eaten. Choose local honey, potatoes, berries foraged from the wild, and nettles picked in spring for soup. Check what's in season and cook accordingly.

- Plan your meals for the week ahead, to avoid waste. Stick to simple meals during the week, including one day for leftovers, and save new or complicated recipes for the weekend, when you have more time.

- Shred and salt your cabbage and make sauerkraut. Store it in jars—a simple way to have fresh vitamin C all year around.

chapter 5

lagom and the home

"A home is not dead, but living, and like
all living things must obey the laws of nature
by constantly changing."

Carl Larsson

seasonal style

The quote by Swedish artist Carl Larsson is very descriptive of how a Swedish home changes throughout the seasons. Carl Larsson and his wife Karin created a style in their home that was to influence twentieth-century Scandinavian design, and it was characterized by unpretentiousness, familiarity and comfort, and lightness.

Beside defining sustainability, frugality, and work/life balance, lagom can also determine the way we live in our homes. Since lagom is about finding a way that works for you and your surroundings, it can easily be applied to the interior of your home, and, in some respects, the exterior, too. In Scandinavia, we live with the seasons and decorate accordingly. The aim is to balance the outside with the inside.

For example, in winter when daylight hours are limited, we make sure we stock up on candles, tealights, and votives. We illuminate dark corners and windows with lamps, either hanging or free standing, and place large lanterns with a candle outside the front door. We may work a bit more, sleep more, and get more settled in our homes, because we know we are going to spend a lot of time there.

Our home is much more than a place to sleep.

Charlotta Anderson, from Hästen Beds in Stockholm, notices a definite, identifiable move toward buying cozy items for the home in the fall. "You see a tendency for nesting — people buy more blankets, decorative cushions/pillows, candles, and things that make the home comfortable and warm. That is the season when people start thinking of buying a new bed." When spring comes, quite the reverse is true. That's when people "wake up" she says. "People want to freshen up their homes by doing a spring clean, changing textiles around, and updating interiors a bit."

The switch with the seasons is pronounced. As the days grow longer, we turn our faces to the sun at any opportunity. We start to seek out the *söderväggen*, an outside wall that faces south, so we can enjoy as much sunlight as possible. Scandinavians live and die by the light! My sister is very good at finding the right spot for the best rays. It's quite a talent.

It feels natural to want to hibernate during the colder and darker season and then to wake up slowly with the sun and recharge your batteries. I don't recall my parents ever updating the wallpaper in our house, although I do remember my mother changing the curtains in the kitchen and living room every spring and fall and of course at Easter and Christmas. In this rather effortless and lagom way, she made the rooms feel fresh and the seasons flowed through with ease. Of course, most people don't have drapes on rotation but there's something quite comforting about updating a few things with the seasons and bringing nature in as it changes outside.

Try this... holly and ivy

This simple idea is a great way to bring nature and coziness into your home.

You will need

long branches of holly, preferably with berries

long stems of ivy

adhesive putty (Blu-Tack), optional

Trail lengths of greenery down the middle of your table and dot tealights/votives in the spaces. In fact, you can decorate as many surfaces as possible with your holly and ivy—tuck it behind paintings and above doorframes; weave it around photos and lamp bases. If you have shelves, rest the holly and ivy along them or, if they won't stay put, use a dab of adhesive putty to hold them down.

lagom with your thermostat

You can ensure your house is intact, safe, and warm with lagom. Draft-proofing and making sure that all your lamps have energy-efficient light bulbs will help you to use electricity in moderation, as will lowering your thermostat and keeping warm by using blankets and sheepskins (there is nothing lagom about being cold). The aim is to strike a balance between comfort and making the changes that can affect your environment in a positive way. We have the power to do our bit. An energy-efficient kettle can save you and the world a lot of electricity. I know not to leave the tap running, but by habit I still sometimes tend to fill the kettle up to the top to boil when I need just one mugful. So rather than fitting in lagom here and there, try adopting it as a whole approach to life and see how the way you think of the environment and the rest of the world in general changes over time.

simplify your style

This idea of moderation can be extended to the way you decorate your house. Perhaps take more of a minimalist approach and style your home a little more sparsely? Actually, minimalist and sparse do not really do justice to the lagom look because those words draw comparisons with austerity whereas the lagom look has to do with striking a balance between wellbeing and sustainability. Natural materials, such as wood, cork, and stone, are key elements. An emphasis on nesting and comfort is also important, so think of textiles such as linen, wool, and woven wallhangings and rugs.

It doesn't matter if you are not an expert in interior decoration. Put the things that you love in pride of place, and pare back accessories and anything that doesn't fit or serve a purpose. In the end, if you can keep your home uncluttered and life simpler than it was before, you can achieve more of what you want, be it time or balance.

Bettina Bieberstein-Lee, Managing Editor at popular Swedish magazine *Lantliv*, explains that for her "lagom is definitely linked to 'good enough,' —you don't have to take things to extremes, whether it's life in general, food, or interiors. The style in Swedish homes is often very natural, even a bit restrained in the best possible sense."

Lagom involves achieving equal measures, be it your time or slices of cake, and she suggests that perhaps "One may not dare to be different,

DO IT YOUR WAY

Sandra Isaksson, a Swedish designer based in the UK, feels that "lagom allows for each individual to decide what is just right for him or her. No one else can define what is your lagom and that is where the true cleverness of lagom comes in."

but there is also a sense of calm to it: you don't fall for trends and fads as easily. Instead, you leave the interior discreet in order to make more room for the people sharing the space, art, and so on."

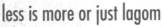

less is more or just lagom

Instead of spending money on several small items that won't last, save up and spend the same amount on a well-designed, good-quality item, perhaps made from sustainable materials, that you can treasure and which will give you a lot of pleasure every time you use it. It can be a cooking pot, a beautiful chair, or a lamp. Per Carlsson, interior designer at JM Construction, agrees that "natural materials, such as linen, leather, stone, and wood, are key. But what is essential is always to think 'sustainable,' and rather than buying lots of things that don't last, focus on items that are of good quality."

My silky gray sheepskin rugs from the Gotland breed of sheep provide a good example. I bought them in Sweden and could have got about four other sheepskin rugs in Ikea for the same price but they wouldn't have been the same. The whole family, including our cat Frida, love them and can't get enough of snuggling up on them. Our rugs are sustainable, natural, and will bring us joy for a very long time.

Of course, not all good things are new. Buying second-hand reduces your carbon footprint and something

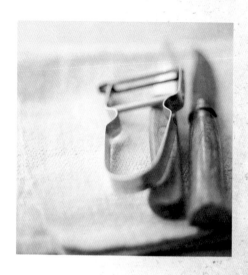

inherited often holds good memories, perhaps a chest that has been passed down through the generations. In my case, it's a cake tin that my mother kept cookies in. Together these things make a living home that reflects the inhabitants. Per Carlsson advises a calm starting point. "What is important is to get a sense of coherence at the base so neither your style nor color palette run away with you. Then add to that base, green plants and flowers, textiles and natural materials, and mix and match new and old, purchased and inherited."

An item that doesn't leave you wanting more, lasts a long time, is functional, and worthy of the space it occupies in your home can be considered lagom. That goes for the way you equip your kitchen, too. Anna Bergenström, the legendary Swedish cookery writer, agrees as she declares that "my recipes should be easy to prepare without unnecessary fuss or gadgets." She explains that in her kitchen she has "three excellent knives, several good chopping boards, a handheld whisk, a food processor, and a hand blender for soup, and more gadgets should not be needed for preparing either simple or more complicated dishes!"

Since our spaces grow smaller, especially in an urban environment,

decluttering is even more important. Curate your belongings and make sure they really earn their space, or you may feel overwhelmed. Having a clean and calm space that is inviting and relaxing is important for your health. Research has shown that women who live in cluttered spaces tend to have higher levels of the stress-related hormone cortisol. What do we do with all our gadgets, for example? Think about how lagom your relationship is with technology.

plant power

I think anyone who lives surrounded by nature will feel more connected to the environment than a town-dweller may feel, and hence more protective toward mother earth. However, most of us live in urban environments, so what can we do to add a touch of the natural world to our lives? An inclination toward house plants may stem from a longing to include something natural as a contrast to an ever faster and unsettled world. Exposure to nature not only makes us feel emotionally more stable but it also contributes to our physical wellbeing. Just watch how cranky children change for the better once they spend time outside. According to scientists at NASA, plants can also improve indoor air quality. Easy-to-grow plants, such as English Ivy (*Hedera helix*), peace lilies (*Spathiphyllum*), and spider plants (*Chlorophytum comosum*), absorb many chemicals and carbon dioxide through pores in their leaves.

A vast body of research exists linking experiences of natural environments with mental health, improved mood, reduced stress and anxiety, and reduced aggression and crime. Perhaps most of us dream of a closer connection to nature in order to bring us a sense of calm, even though a move out of town is neither possible nor practical. As Bettina Bieberstein-Lee explains, "even though many people dream of a sustainable and wholesome lifestyle in the countryside, you don't necessarily need to become a full-time farmer to achieve that. Instead, realize your dreams by being a bit more lagom, living sustainably, and using plants and natural materials to adorn your home."

Think of each item's journey. Where did it come from, who made it, what resources were used to create it?

BRING NATURE INSIDE

Throughout the year, my family loves to bring nature into the home. We plant bulbs in terra-cotta pots, usually paperwhites (*Narcissus papyraceus*). At the start of spring, we collect twigs in bud, including species of willow (*Salix*) with soft catkins, arrange them in a vase, and watch the leaves come out. At Easter time, we bring in vast bunches of twigs from the common birch tree and decorate them with feathers and eggs. When I was growing up, my parents didn't stop at twigs. They used to bring in a whole birch tree. In fact, the row of birch trees on our street was a determining factor in my decision to buy our house. Throughout summer, there is always something blooming in a vase somewhere in the house, and by the time fall rolls around, sparkling colors abound — rowanberries, branches with maple leaves, rosehips, English ivy. I make a wreath of colorful leaves to hang on our door, and perhaps even have a go at making a mandala out of them, among other treasures. For winter, and Christmas, we bring in pine cones, and make a branch from pine and dried oranges (as they are in season), and plant up bulbs of hyacinths and amaryllis to scent the house.

Try this... seasonal wreaths

Wreaths are lovely at any time of year. You can hang them on the front door or have them inside—lying on the table with a candle in the center, if you like. The twig frame will last for ages and all you have to do is replace the flowers and leaves when they start to fade.

You will need

45–50 inch/120–130 cm lengths of ash, beech, or willow twigs, stripped of their side branches, at least 10

secateurs/pruning shears

string, green twine, or raffia cut into 1 yard/ 1 m lengths

seasonal flowers and leaves with stems as long as possible

other decorations— you choose

florist's wire, cut into 6 inch/15 cm lengths

Take half the twigs firmly in one hand, as if they were a bunch of flowers. Wrap string or raffia around the base of the bunch several times and tie the string in a firm knot. Add the rest of the twigs near the top of the first bunch, securing it in the same way, and then bend the twigs around in a circle. (It can take a few

attempts to get this right.) Wrap string or raffia around the frame several times and tie in a firm knot to hold the twigs together securely. Do this in several places.

Thread in long-stemmed flowers and leaves, weaving the stems in and out of the twig frame.

Instead of flowers (or as well as) you could use fruit, chili peppers, pine cones, or bundles of cinnamon sticks, and anything else suitable you have at hand. To attach decorations such as shells (with holes drilled in them) and baubles, center the decoration on a short piece of florist's wire, twist both ends of the wire together two or three times just above the decoration, wrap the wire around the frame, and secure by twisting the ends together again. To attach fruit, such as apples or oranges, skewer the fruit with a short length of florist's wire, wrap the wire ends around the frame, and then twist them together to secure.

If you always have an extra something natural in your house, mixing it with plants already in pots, you will increase harmony and lower stress levels.

the lagom way...
how to bring lagom into your home

- Scale back your possessions. Remove one thing from each room every week for a few months and notice how your energy lifts. By having less stuff, you will have more time to live your life in the way you want to. Harmony and balance is very lagom.

- If you add an item, make it something that is not only beautiful but also functional and well made. Look on Etsy for handmade items, seek out your local craft fair to discover new artists and makers, and look at what you already have in your house.

- Bring the outside in. Focus on natural and sustainable materials, such as wood, wool, and metal, and introduce plants here and there. Ask people for cuttings, and share if you have some. Collect twigs, acorns, driftwood, stones from the beach to anchor you in nature.

- Don't overcomplicate. Keep things simple. One new thing in, two things out.

chapter 6

lagom and the body

All things in moderation and
moderation in all things.

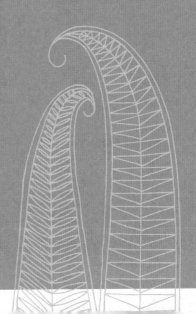

enjoy keeping fit

The Swedish-style aerobic exercise *friskis* and *svettis* is lagom through and through and the great thing about it is that everyone can join in. It really is the simplest of ideas. It started in 1978 in Stockholm with the goal that everyone should be able to find their way to exercise, and not much has changed since.

Kia Duncan, a *friskis* and *svettis* trainer in London, explains that *friskis medel jympa* (medium aerobics) is lagom exercise exemplified. "We exercise, have fun, and socialize at the same time. Anyone can join in and no one sticks out, from the young Swedish au pair to the retired old French man, and no one bats an eyelid. You don't have to be superfit or able to coordinate your limbs or remember long choreographies. You just jump around to the music and have fun, with the added bonus of exercise."

"Jump around to the music and have fun" is something I could sign up for, and especially since I don't think lycra is required. Unfortunately, from a way of keeping fit, exercise can turn into something extreme. Social-media pages are full of selfies of people in the gym, on the running track, and on the yoga mat, giving the impression that everyone is exercise mad and looking wonderful as a result. What starts as an innocent, and praiseworthy, attempt to get fit can lead to something unhealthy and damaging, causing you more stress. In Sweden, where lagom is the backbone to how we live our lives and make decisions, we don't seem to adopt the same approach to fitness and health, which has always surprised me.

Elina Sundström, author of the book *Hälsohets (Health Stress)* thinks the fact that we are logged on to the web so often is causing us to take health information beyond lagom. She says, "Swedes are very conscious of news regarding health, illnesses, and environment, and therefore we also absorb any wellness trends extremely quickly."

This has seemingly translated into a very un-lagom trend of following punishing training schedules to achieve better results, and imposing unrealistic demands on ourselves to be more efficient and streamlined in our fitness regimes.

While there is something admirable about training hard to improve fitness levels, there is a fine line between that and pushing yourself into extremes. As soon as it starts taking too much time away from things you love and enjoy, you might want to ask yourself if that is really lagom. Following a lifestyle that is centered around balance and moderation is a great way to keep your stress levels in check.

Elina Sundström reflects that in a fast-changing world, and in societies where the extended family unity is fragmented, the main things we have some kind of control over are health, exercise, and work. "There seems to be some kind of collective performance-based self-esteem," she says, "so we are defined by what we do and not by who we are, which results in rest and recuperation being seen as unnecessary. We always have to be 'doing' something useful in order not to be wasting time."

exercise the lagom way

Somewhere among all of this we seem to have lost a way of knowing when things are balanced. We leave a demanding workplace and go straight to the gym where again we have to achieve targets and improve our performance. Instead of a relaxing end to the day, it becomes another place to compete, and that can reduce the good effects of exercise and moving the body. The Goldilocks effect, coined by Amy Arnsten, states that the brain needs balance and so when the brain gets knocked sideways by having too many demands made of it, it starts misfiring and overreacting. So think lagom next time and consider whether a quiet time at home and an early night might give you more benefit than an evening spent at the gym.

Elina Sundström believes that even though we try to find lagom in our lives, sometimes we get it wrong. "The term lagom can be pushed over the edge, or too much or too little, and that doesn't do us any good at all. We need to take responsibility for our lives and our health instead of following a trend that influences how we think we should live."

Lagom fun, lagom exercise, lagom with social interaction—an activity that doesn't take up too much of your time. Wonderful!

FIND YOUR OWN PATH

Boel Stier, founder of Miro Publishing and the force behind the Health for Wealth podcast, expands on the idea that living in an unsettled world drives people to find foundations to hold on to, especially in secularized societies. She speculates "that perhaps the big interest in food, wellness, and health has become a substitute for something spiritual. To influence how we eat and keep fit is a way to contribute to a better world both for you as an individual and for the environment as a whole. It's a way to find meaning."

Instead of tyrannically sticking to a regime, take a moment—take many moments—every day to check in with yourself. When you do that regularly, you can start to understand yourself and your reactions to things and what really matters to you. Sundström also points out that "your lagom changes during the years, so it's important to check/measure what you need right there and then to reduce the risk of poor health and improve your chances of feeling good and having energy."

everyday opportunities

Lagom is about enjoying experiences during everyday life. Could you combine your need for movement with something else? Try taking time to walk around during your lunch break. Walk home through the park even if it's a bit farther. Organize a weekend walk with your friends and combine it with lunch. If you like to run, that can do wonders for your mental clarity and your general mood but only if you don't overdo it.

My mother, born 1930, is still a very fit and strong individual. Beside stretching or gentle yoga classes, which she took up in her later years, she has never done what we would classify as exercise. She does, on the other hand, go for walks, work in the garden, take the wheelbarrow to the dump, dig up potatoes, and mow the lawn.

Parkrun was set up back in 2004 in London and there are now over one million participants all over the world. The concept is simple and it's organized by volunteers. You turn up every Saturday or Sunday and run 5k, and it doesn't

Semi strenuous, everyday tasks, performed regularly,
can keep you fit and healthy.

This is my mother working on the vegetable patch—
left, around 40 years ago, and right, today!

WALK CROSS-COUNTRY

One of the best ways to take exercise must be with a group of people in nature. Nordic Walking originated in Finland when cross-country skiers wanted to find a way of keeping fit in the off season and came up with the idea of walking with poles. Other people realized the value of the technique and Nordic Walking clubs can now be found all over the world. Old and young meet for cross-country walks to get fit and enjoy nature.

matter how fast you go. What matters is taking part in something fun. The exercise is an added extra — just like with *friskis* and *svettis*. You might even make new friends. The point is inclusiveness and wellbeing.

The trend for finding more balance in the way we take exercise is probably welcomed by many. Mikkeller brewery in Copenhagen started a running club a few years back and the idea has spread to more than a hundred cities across the world. You may wonder at a brewery starting a running club. How does that work? The members meet, run, and then go for a few beers together. To help find the balance between drinking and running, Mikkeller set up an app so members can keep track of beer consumption balanced against distance run. It's also a way to keep in touch with other runners. The combination of physical exertion and indulgence could be a great way of finding your lagom in life, especially if you have a tendency to go overboard with physical exercise or new "clean eating" habits. As well as keeping you motivated, being in a group puts a smile on your face and adds value to your life with the social connection.

good lagom, good skin, clean house

If you can find your mental balance and manage your stress levels, it will be evident not only in your ability to make good decisions and think clearly but in your skin, too. Balance is key and if that is disturbed, it will show up in the largest organ of your body, the skin. In looking after yourself, often the simple things are best — enough sleep, good whole foods, sunlight, fresh air, and a straightforward skin-care routine. Choose products with a short ingredients list, or make your own. The human body is an effective machine and everything is connected, so it will find a way to communicate when the equilibrium is upset. All we have to do is teach ourselves how to listen to it.

The same care should be taken when choosing products to clean your house — think natural to avoid toxic fumes. *Såpa* is an all-natural product made in Sweden from liquid rosin. It's been used for hundreds of years and I can't remember my mother ever using anything else to clean the house. It's so lagom — it cleans as well as any of the other products that line our shelves and it's also good for the environment. At a push, you can even wash your clothes or oil your bike chain with it. If you can't get hold of it, use a mixture of distilled white vinegar, bicarbonate of soda, water, and castile spray (a biodegradable liquid soap), and apply with a microfiber cloth.

Another old trick to use to remove smells from the fridge is to place a cut-up lemon in it. The lemon can also be used for getting sinks sparkling white.

These suggestions are not to do with being frugal but everything to do with

being sensible. Why use a smelly, toxic solution that pollutes our environment — and you probably won't be able to recycle the empty container — when you can use something that is good for both your health and the rest of the world? It doesn't make sense. There is nothing lagom about it at all.

> "There is no such thing as bad clothes, only bad weather"—Swedish saying

lagom and clothes

Scandis generally stay away from brand logos and obvious trends and, as far as colors are concerned, stick to grays and earthy tones. The lagom mentality explains why we are drawn toward measured and muted clothes above more ostentatious and louder styles. No one likes a show off, especially in Scandinavia. It is a good idea to regard texture as if it was a color—mix wools, fine knits, silk, and cottons—and think about cuts and shapes.

The lagom way means choosing the right clothes for the weather. There is nothing stylish about getting dressed up if you are going to be cold. However, stylishness need not be lost just because you are being sensible. Think layers, layers, and more layers.

In Sweden, everyone is prepared for any kind of weather and has all the right gear. When my children were small we went to the park most days, no matter the weather. The rainy days were the most fun. We were kitted out in rubber boots and all-in-one waterproofs and if there were others in the park, you could bet your life that 99 percent of them were fellow Scandinavians. It was easy to spot them by their sensible outdoor gear.

When visiting home, I often underestimate the weather. It can be so cold in Sweden, and not having a warm enough jacket or shoes can ruin your day, as

THINK SUBTLE

It's fine to jazz up outfits with accessories but don't wear them all at once. Think balance. Even though Sweden is the third largest exporter of music behind the UK and US, we have yet to produce a hip hop artist, which might have something to do with the bling. Bling is very un-lagom.

can being dressed inappropriately for a freak warm day in April. There is always an outfit that is lagom for the weather. If you have the right clothes, you can spend more time outside, comfortably. Open-air culture, *friluftsliv* (free air life), is a way of life in Scandinavia and it permeates the early years of school. A forest school teacher told me that they are out in *ur och skur* (all weather) and take refuge indoors only in a snow storm or when the temperature drops below minus ten. She pointed out that the kids were rarely off sick. Their "indoors" was a large military-style tent. When the young ones needed a nap, they slept in there on beds made from pine branches and sheepskin. You bet those kids had the best outdoor gear and were never too cold, too wet, or too warm — or cranky.

the lagom way...
how to be lagom about your body

🌿 Be more relaxed about a fitness routine and don't overdo it. There is a time to rest, to work, and to move. Find way a way to exercise that adds value to your life. Take a solo run to clear your head or go with an organized group to be sociable.

🌿 Be lagom about searching for balance. Accept that there will always be imbalance in your life. Some days you work more and that is what you do on that day. Some days you have time to work out. Try not to compartmentalize every hour of your life. Go with the flow.

🌿 Keep things simple. Use natural beauty products in moderation. As far as skin is concerned, easy does it—good food, relaxation, and fresh air usually take care of the rest.

🌿 Buy some good-quality outdoor gear so you don't have an excuse for not getting out in all kinds of weathers. If you have kids, kit them out properly, too, so they can be comfortable outdoors, you don't have worry about mud and rain, and everyone is happy.

chapter 7

lagom and the wider world

Lagom, a way of finding inner peace through moderation and inclusion, is a very attractive proposition in a world that seems hell bent on excess and division.

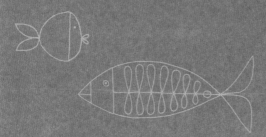

fair shares

The way we think about food, shopping, styling our home, grooming, growing our own, and never taking the last *kanelbulle* (cinnamon roll) on the plate can be translated into the wider world. While lagom is about where you as an individual find your balance in life and where your idea of "just right" fits in, the sentiment behind how you incorporate it in everyday life can work on a bigger scale. The products and food you buy, and your behavior, impact on the climate and environment—having the right light bulbs, for example, and not leaving the tap running. Sensible practices such as these show consideration for the rest of the world and contribute to improving it—taking what you need and leaving enough for everyone else.

A wonderful example of how inclusion and moderation work on the big scale is the Swedish *allemansrätten* (freedom to roam). This gives people the right to explore nature without asking permission from the landowner, providing they don't act irresponsibly. It's summed up in the phrase "don't disturb, don't destroy"—not a bad mantra for life in general. It is a law that has emerged from people's custom of enjoying the outdoors, and it is even mentioned twice in legislation that everyone has the right to spend time in nature. Many Swedes consider the freedom to roam to be a human right and to put up a "no trespassing" sign could be considered a violation.

"The Swedish *allemansrätten* makes it easy for people to access nature every day," says Per Nilson from the Swedish Environmental Protection Agency. "They

can take a walk, go for a run, bring the buggy. It makes people healthier since it allows for an easy way to get out and about, and experiencing nature is then a much simpler task."

The approach to life based on sustainability, moderation, and living in a healthy balance with the rest of the world can be likened to the concept that economists call "declining marginal utility," which is often used to explain consumer demands. Put simply, as we consume more of a service or goods, the additional benefits decline. So, for example, if you have ten apples, with each apple you eat the desire to eat another one declines and eventually you reach saturation point. The more resources, such as time and money, we consume, the nearer we get to saturation point. But if everyone consumes in moderation, that would maximize the benefits and leave enough for everyone. A very lagom approach I think we can agree.

This could be applied to employee policies and working hours — each additional hour you work beyond a regular day adds less to your output and productivity. If workers are allowed shorter working days, staff happiness may increase and that could have a significant effect on a range of variables within that company, such as efficiency and production as a whole.

In her book *Ten Thoughts on Time*, published in 1999, physicist Professor Bodil Jönsson reflected on how our lives are ruled by the clock and even though we are living longer than we used to, we feel we have less time. Recently, she published another book in which she puts forward a different way of looking at the hours we work, proposing that they should reflect what phase of life we are

WORKPLACE EQUALITY

Sweden is a high-trust society. We feel that the government is more of a friend than a foe, and looks after our best interests so we can live the life we want. Better working conditions with job equality and strong working unions have led to a less hierarchical structure in the workplace than in some other countries. When I arrived in the UK, I was surprised at the strong emphasis placed on the boss and the division between employees. In Sweden, no one is really put on a pedestal. Everyone, regardless of age, social class, and gender, is addressed informally, and it's not uncommon to have direct contact with the bosses, which means that structures are in place to get your voice heard when necessary. For a Scandinavian, the many layers of management in a company elsewhere, and the strict rules on how you communicate, can come as a shock.

in. Working hours, she suggests, should be divided up so parents have time to look after small children, look out for teenagers, or care for elderly relatives. These things should be taken into consideration and working hours shared around, depending on what stage we are at in life. When working time is limited for some, others will be able to work for longer. Elina Sundström, yogi and author of the book *Hälsohets (Health Stress)*, points out that "lagom working hours for some can be sixty hours a week and twenty hours for someone else."

Of course, it's up to us to take responsibility for how we live our lives and how that impacts on the rest of the world. However, Elina Sundström says that employers also need to step up and offer the right conditions so that "people can have a more lagom life … live more balanced and sustainable [lives]."

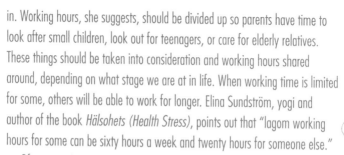

Thinking of the group as a whole may partly explain why Scandinavian countries often end up in the top league in the happiness index.

culture of the collective

Perhaps due to a lagom mentality, Swedes can take a long time to make a decision because we have to seek everyone's opinion. Try choosing a movie with a bunch of Swedes. It can take a while. We expect discussions to be clear and open and everyone to have an equal say — just don't flap your hands around or raise your voice while saying it. I know a few Brits, including my husband, who have been surprised with an apology from a Swede after an evening spent chatting over a few beers. What the Brit thought was a healthy exchange of views the Swede took very differently, waking up next day full of remorse and worry that their relationship had been irrevocably ruined.

Since everyone has to be consulted, family decisions can take a long time, too. When my entire family are gathered, there are a lot of us, and going for a walk can turn into a major operation. I will say to my husband, Oliver, "We're going for a walk," so he puts on his jacket and shoes, as any normal person would, and goes outside, ready to roll. Quite a while later he will ask if we're still going for a walk. Yes of course, but first we have to check if Y wants to come and she is on the phone right now. X says she is coming but first she has to hang up the washing and Z is meeting us halfway but we must go by a certain route so as not to miss her and my mother is looking for her walking boots, which she thinks are up in the loft, and perhaps we will just have some fika before we set off while we wait for Y and X ... and on it goes. By the time everyone is ready, my dear husband will often have set off on his own.

lagom and relationships

When you grow up in a large family, negotiating in a kind way and considering other people's feelings is important so that everyone can get along, and relationships are kept at a lagom level. You would never dream of taking the last cookie on the plate. If there are not enough for everyone to have seconds, what is left will be divided up. This comes as second nature and, in a way, is how Swedish society functions as a whole, and can be translated into a bigger picture of how to behave lagom.

At 19, I moved abroad, as a very innocent and somewhat sheltered Swede, and was surprised at how many fractured families I heard about in my new global friendship group. ("What, you mean you actually don't like your sister?") Perhaps that is when I started to appreciate the lagom approach to relationships.

Competition and rivalry in all its manifestations are usually put forward positively as healthy and developmental for the majority of individuals and for society. They influence many areas including sport, television, workplaces, and schools, and have almost become an ideology in themselves. This trend, mainly among the younger generation, has created a layer of society in which people think more of the individual than of society as a whole.

However, Eva-Lotta Hulten, in her recently published book *Klara Färdiga Gå (Ready, Steady, Go)*, explores the idea that competition can be harmful, and turning people into rivals instead of potential co-workers can leave us beset by feelings of worthlessness and loneliness. Lagom is about compassion for your

fellow man and I think that is what's needed right now in the world, and what many people are striving for. I believe it can ultimately make you happier.

Researcher Sonja Lyubomirsky found out to her surprise what made happy people happy and unhappy people unhappy. She interviewed "extremely happy and extremely unhappy" people and it turned out that the happy people made comparisons by their own personal "happy gauge" and not by measuring the level of their happiness compared to others who were worse off. This was surprising to the team because they also found that the happy people felt pleased for those who succeeded and compassion for those who didn't. The individualism that allows us to make our own decisions is healthy for us, but the kind that puts us against each other makes us feel pain. There is something very lagom about this way of thinking.

SING, SING, SING

According to the Swedish choir union, about 600,000 Swedes sing in a choir, and while that may not seem like a lot, it actually makes Sweden the country with the highest number of choirs *per capita* in the world. Research has shown that singing in a choir can bring a lot of happiness and numerous health benefits. In a survey conducted by Oxford Brookes University, in England, to find out who were the happiest, people who sang in choirs, sang alone, or played team sports, the choristers came out on top. They thought of the choir as their "team" but the added benefit was that they regarded the activity as "meaningful." Possibly the cohesiveness of the activity and its non-competitive nature had something to do with it, too. Swedish research found that singing in a group released oxytocin, the happy hormone, which lowers stress levels and blood pressure. Perhaps the growth in choirs stems from a desire for a community as our society has become increasingly fragmented and fractured. Singing with a group is something that you can just do and be yourself.

lagom and connection

The benefits of nature, gardening, and growing-your-own are well documented. I know how they can bring general peace and contentment, having re-established closer contact with nature later on in life. A study made at Plymouth University, England showed that allotment/community gardening has a positive impact on health and wellbeing, mentally as well as physically. Social connection with individuals, sharing thoughts, ideas, and skills in a natural environment, contributes to stress reduction.

If we can be in touch with nature in some form, be it by having indoor plants, a garden, or the forest by the backdoor, the benefits are enormous. The more contact you have with the natural world the more you understand this, especially if you experience it from a young age.

Per Nilson says, "The freedom to roam is built on showing respect for nature, landowners, and other people encountered in the countryside, and I like to compare it to one giant democratic project. Everyone can join in but you have to show care and consideration. Sometimes it doesn't work as certain people want to take a larger piece of the cake."

What could be more lagom than that, because if we don't look after our environment and care for our fellow man, there might not be anywhere left to roam. The sooner we all apply a little bit of lagom to our daily lives, the more likely it is that we can all enjoy more of this freedom.

Try this... floating ferns

These fern circles don't require too much effort to make and are a lovely way to keep in touch with nature. They last just a few days, so make several in different diameters and keep on replacing them. The circles are easier to make in spring when the fronds are young and less prone to snapping as you bend them. Choose ferns with pliable fronds and plenty of evenly spaced leaves. If you're finding them hard to bend, take a sharp knife and score the whole way down the back of the stem.

You will need

4 fern fronds (the longer, the better)

green floristry stub wire

garden clippers (secateurs)

metal circular wreath

fishing wire

Starting at the stalk end of one frond, wrap stub wire over and around the base of each leaf and around the metal circle. Wrap the wire around tightly, keeping it as close to the circle as possible so there are no gaps. Stop winding just before you reach the tip of the frond.

Start again with a new frond, making sure you tuck the beginning of it under the tip of the frond you've wired. Keep going until you've covered the whole circle in ferns. Cut off any protruding pieces of wire. Attach a length of fishing wire to the top of the circle and suspend it in the window or wherever you like.

Try this... forsythia arrangement

You will need

sycamore blossom
and leaves

forsythia stems

hawthorn stems

old bucket (or another
suitable container)

Forsythia appears before many of the other
spring-flowering shrubs and it can be picked while
the flowers are still lime-green. Bring it inside so
you can watch it blossom. It lasts for ages. If you
can find some other twigs, branches, and blossom,
such as sycamore or hawthorn, you can make an
unusual and instantly attractive arrangement—a
lovely way to bring nature into the home and a
smile to everyone's face.

Cut all the stems on the
diagonal, then plunge 10 per
cent of the length of the stem
into boiling water for 20
seconds.

Fill the bucket with cold water
and start adding the stems
without blossom first.

As you add the forsythia and
other finds, stand back every so
often to make sure you're happy
with the shape the arrangement
is taking.

the lagom way...
how to be more lagom in your view of the wider world

꙳ Try to change your mindset about the implications of your actions, and truly believe that your small changes can make a difference in the wider world.

꙳ Next time you have a discussion with someone you don't agree with, try the lagom approach and allow for compromise. Different opinions can co-exist alongside each other.

꙳ Recycle. Even better, try to avoid buying things with a lot of packaging so you have less to recycle. Buy only what you need. That way you save resources on so many levels.

꙳ Join a choir or another group where you can share your interest. The more you start relating to people as a collective, full of joy and plain old humanity rather than as pesky individuals, the more compassion and understanding of the wider world you may feel. No research to back that up. Just a thought that comes from being lagom for most of my life.

꙳ Get your kids out in nature at an early age to instil in them a respect for the environment and the world we live in.

lagom and the soul

Only you know how to find balance and inner
knowledge, and by simply staying quiet, both
metaphorically and literally, you will learn
to let it in.

ever-changing lagom

When I was growing up, I sometimes found everyone else's idea of what was "just right" to be a bit dull, which made me question why my level of lagom was outside the consensus of the group. Now I can see how the concept can be applied to so many situations in life. Deep down, we all have a lagom gauge that can tell us where our level of lagom lies.

"I once heard a Buddhist teacher say that 'balance is not a static act,'" says Linn from Straightforward Nutrition. Linn is a nutritional therapist from Sweden, based in Ireland, who helps people heal their relationship with food, through mindful eating and self-compassion. "This is what I have learned for myself, too," she continues. "My lagom is ever changing, and the best way to find that balance of just enough is to listen closely to what my body is telling me, and then act accordingly, whether that is to rest when I'm tired or eat when I'm hungry. Only you can know what your lagom is. Dare to be courageous and trust that your body carries that wisdom. All you have to do is tap into it."

However, it's one thing to measure how much to eat and drink, but it takes a bit of soul searching to learn what portion sizes you want out of life. We all know when we have bitten off more than we can chew, and we also know when it's the other way around. Somewhere in between those two, there's a time to ask yourself, "Is this just about right? Is this lagom?"

find the balance

We all take different journeys to reach calmness and balance. Some people find that meditating helps them to know where to draw the line in their lives. Others who find meditating a bit tricky (me included) may prefer to find their peace by getting out in nature, practicing yoga, or having some time for themselves. I find I'm better at tuning in to myself in those quiet moments, and recognizing "just right" — nothing less, nothing more, just lagom. I can say no to more activities when I know my weekend is already lagom busy, realize when I haven't had enough lagom exercise that week, and understand when it's a lagom time to leave the party (one I admit I have never been very good at).

It's a case of knowing when to stop — not going overboard with gardening, for example — realizing when you are actually content and not going after more, which is a natural thing for human beings to do but doesn't always lead to more happiness. Perhaps the world needs a new word to express "enough" or "sufficient," because these and similar words imply a lack of something or that you have to give up some things to maintain balance, but lagom doesn't mean either of those. Lagom doesn't mean perfect, either — it means perfect with regard to the circumstances.

Your lagom might be taking the time to walk through the park on your way to the station or searching out some greenery on your lunch break. Imagine a connection with the roots of a tree and consider that, whatever happens in your life, nature carries on regardless, following the yearly cycle. An old saying springs to mind: "Half of whatever you worry about doesn't happen and half of it happens anyway, so why worry?" Somewhere in that wise statement, you can find a lagom approach—worry a little bit but at the same time remember that fretting is no use. If you do find yourself getting too anxious, perhaps it's time to sit down for some fika or to take a walk in the park to try to reach some understanding of what lagom worry really entails for you.

stop at lagom

Ultimately, lagom is about making sure that there is enough for all of us—enough cake, enough nature, enough resources, just the right amount of inclusion so that people don't feel left out, enough politeness while maintaining lagom directness and honesty. One of the myths about where the word lagom comes from is based on the old Swedish farming society when people were getting by on very little. If someone improved his family's living standards, the consequence was that others had less. Being lagom about your wants meant showing consideration to your neighbors, so no one person would end up worse off.

THE EFFECT OF NATURE

Instead of visiting church on Sundays, it has been said that Swedes often search for spirituality in nature, although we might not actually call it this because that would be almost like showing off. It's just a walk in the woods with some fika and perhaps a small bucket brought along for foraging purposes. The fact that we may find peace while listening to the sound of the wind in the tall pine trees, bird song, or the silence while we sip our coffee is just a side thing. You could draw parallels between the Scandinavians' reverence for the spiritual element of nature and the way Native Americans respect it and find it sacred. We all live in nature and we are also a part of it. If we can show this to our children, we will be passing on our cultural heritage.

Perhaps by applying the lagom principle to our world and our society we could see changes. By finding more contentment, be it by spending time in nature or at weekly choir practice, assigning time to the things we really value in life, which make us happy, we may be more likely to be generous with compassion, understanding, and space. Swedish comedian Jonas Gardell, who was distinctly un-lagom when he first made an appearance, was asked how he dared to stand up alone on stage in front of thousands of people. "It's not me against all of the audience," he responded. "It's all of us together." Perhaps, with a viewpoint like that, it's easier to remember that not everything is a big competition.

Imagine if this sort of thinking could translate to a bigger scale. People would find more pleasure in simple things and not have such a constant, aching, unsustainable desire for more than they really need, or think they need, in order to be happy. By stopping at lagom, we could achieve a lot.

resources

1000 Hours Outside
www.1000hoursoutside.com This is a global movement focused on matching kids' and adults' screentime with time spent outside enjoying nature. The website has various activities and handy printouts. There is also a shop with lots of cool outdoor stuff and printable curriculums.

Alice in Scandiland
www.aliceinscandiland.com Lovely online shop selling Scandi-style homewares.

Allotments *allotment-garden.org*
Great online learning resource for all things allotment, and a helpful forum, too.

American Community Gardening Association *communitygarden.org*
Promotes and supports all aspects of community gardening, food growing, urban forestry, and greening open spaces.

Brita Sweden *britasweden.se* A Swedish
company selling sustainable plastic rugs and runners and wool blankets. Plastic rugs have been woven in Sweden for many generations and, to me, one of these is the perfect lagom interior item. Practical, stylish, it can be used outdoors and indoors.

Children and Nature Network
childrenandnature.org Connects children, families, and communities to nature.

Community Supported Agriculture UK
communitysupportedagriculture.org.uk

Friskis & Svettis *friskissvettis.co.uk*
Swedish relaxed exercise club.

Gartur Stitch Farm *garturstitchfarm.com*
A great selection of online courses ranging from sourdough baking to creating your own natural home and body care products. There is also a beautiful quarterly magazine focusing on slow, seasonal living

Geoffrey and Grace *geoffreyandgrace. com* A lovely blog embracing a creative and wholehearted approach to life.

The Grey Sheep *thegreysheep.co.uk*
Online shop that sells yarn from Gotland sheep.

Guerrilla Gardening
guerrillagardening.org

Local Harvest *localharvest.org*
A website for locating your nearest Community Supported Agriculture in USA.

London Freedom Seed Bank
www.londonfreedomseedbank.org A network of London-based food growers and gardeners dedicated to saving, storing, and sharing open-pollinated seed.

Love Food Hate Waste
lovefoodhatewaste.com Tips on rethinking your meal planning and using up leftovers.

Mikkeller Running Club
mikkellerrunningclub.dk Running and cycling clubs across the world.

The National Allotment Society
nsalg.org.uk

Nordic Walking *nordicwalking.co.uk*

Park Run *parkrun.com* A series of 5k park runs held across the world. See website for locations and details.

Patch *www.patchplants.com* Houseplants, pots, and growing tips.

Scandi Kitchen *scandikitchen.co.uk* A shop for all things foodie-Scandinavian.

Skandium *skandium.com* Shop selling Nordic homewares.

Sustainable Food Trust *sustainablefoodtrust.org* Organization for sustainable food and farming systems.

Swedish Environmental Protection Agency *www.naturvardsverket.se* Information about the right to roam and the environment in Sweden and abroad.

Vital Seeds *vitalseeds.co.uk* Organic seeds for vegetables, herbs, and flowers.

World Wide Fund for Nature *wwf.org.uk* Leading international nature conservation organization.

Books, Magazines, and Films
91 Magazine 91magazine.co.uk
Just Breathe Magazine justbreathemag.com
The Minimalists: Less is Now, Matt D'Avella for Netflix
Ten Thoughts about Time (UK) / *Unwinding the Clock* (US), Bodil Jönsson
Willpower: Why Self-Control is the Secret to Success, Roy. F. Baumeister and John Tierney

picture credits

acknowledgments

A huge thank you to my beautiful children Alvar, Clara, and Iris and my husband Oliver for putting up with mummy, headphones on, tapping away on the laptop. I couldn't have done it without you. You mean everything to me. Love always.

Thanks to my wonderful family and friends in Sweden, giving me their idea of what lagom is and helping me with suggestions about what is a lagom recipe! Thanks also to Liz, Anja, Erica, and Siobhan for all your encouraging words, support, and lending of Scandi props. Huge thanks also to my friend Ann, her lovely boy Max, and her mother Unni for a fun day, and for helping to set the lagom scene in my little house here in London.

Thanks to CICO Books—to Cindy for taking a chance on me, Pete for the suggestion, and Carmel and Sally for their hard work and endless patience with all my questions. Thank you to Gavin Kingcome for beautiful photography and Nel Haynes for clever styling, to Stephen Conroy, Tonia Shuttleworth, and Tamara Vos for the food photography, to Louise Leffler for her design, and to Marion Paull and Gillian Haslam for their editing.